EYES OF BLOOD

Glitter books

EYES OF BLOOD

ISBN 978-1-902588-24-7

Published 2012 by Glitter Books

Written by Jack Hunter; a version of this book was previously published under the title "Lips Of Blood"

CULT MOVIE FILES

foreword

From Bela Lugosi to Gary Oldman, cinema has seen a huge succession of screen Draculas. Yet none have ever equalled the power, charisma and feral magnetism of Christopher Lee, who first claimed the role in Hammer's 1958 classic **Dracula**, and went on to make it his own over the course of a further six films between then and 1973. When we think of Dracula, we think of Christopher Lee.

Despite growing dissatisfaction with the role, particularly with regard his dialogue (or lack of it), Lee took his portrayal to successively more intense and almost satanic heights, personifying a terrifyingly seductive charge of sex and death which burned from the screen into his audiences' mind's eye. All this beneath an outwardly urbane, austere and disdainful veneer which at first glance belied the beast within. Physically perfect to the point of beauty, elegant yet clearly capable of unleashing psychopathic carnage, Christopher Lee's Dracula remains a consummate creation, and one which ranks amongst the very few most memorable in the history of cinema, on a par with Karloff's Frankenstein monster or Anthony Hopkins's Hannibal Lecter as an iconographic avatar of our collective subconscious.

Eyes Of Blood is an extensive visual and verbal tribute to Lee's Dracula, an overdue recognition of one of the great screen-acting achievements. It also serves to commemorate seven movies which remain amongst the very best made by Hammer Films, and acts as a flash-frozen document of an era and style of cinema which will never be repeated.

EYES OF BLOOD

THE HAMMER FILMS "DRACULA" CYCLE
STARRING CHRISTOPHER LEE

CULT MOVIE FILES

DRACULA

DRACULA (1958)

(US: **Horror Of Dracula**)

Dir: Terence Fisher. Sc: Jimmy Sangster, from the novel by Bram
Stoker. Ph: Jack Asher. Art dir: Bernard Robinson. Ed: Jimmy Needs,
Bill Lenny. Mus: James Bernard. Prod: Anthony Hinds. Rel: Universal
(Britain: through Rank). 82 mins. Eastman Colour.

W: Peter Cushing (Dr. Van Helsing), Christopher Lee (Count Dracula),
Michael Gough (Arthur), Melissa Stribling (Mina), Carol Marsh (Lucy),
Olga Dickie (Gerda), John Van Eyssen (Jonathan Harker), Valerie
Gaunt (Vampire Woman).

SYNOPSIS

Hammer's **Dracula** opens to a shot of a stone eagle and an
ominous, clashing soundtrack. As the credits roll the camera
pans to a castle crypt and a great stone tomb marked simply
"DRACULA". Vivid blood splashes over the nameplate; fade-
out.

The next scene features narration from the diary of
Jonathan Harker. The year is 1885 and Harker is journeying
from the middle European village of klausenberg to the nearby
castle of Count Dracula, where he has secured the position of
librarian. The coachman drops him short of his destination, and
he walks the rest of the way. Finding the castle deserted,
dinner laid out for him and a note of apology from his new
employer, he sits down to eat. Soon he is interrupted by the
arrival of a voluptuous young woman dressed all in white, who
begs him to help her escape from the castle, where she says she
is a prisoner. But she runs off when a shadowy figure appears
appears at the top of the stairs. The figure swiftly descends the
stairs and introduces himself as Dracula. He is an elegant,

handsome, clean-cut aristocratic figure, a perfect physical specimen. Dracula sees Harker to his room; there, he notices a photograph of Harker's fiancée, Lucy, and at once appears abnormally interested in the young woman's image.

The next narrated diary entry reveals Harker's true reason for being at the castle; having infiltrated its walls, he is now secretly bent on destroying its owner, Count Dracula, and his "reign of terror". No further details are specified at this point.

We next find Harker searching the castle. Once again he is approached by the mysterious women in white, who implores him to help her. As he comforts the woman, she starts to eye his throat, and raise her head as if to bite him. She is halted by the abrupt entrance of Dracula. This is a different Dracula to the earlier, urbane host; now his eyes blaze red like an animal's, and his lips are streaked with fresh blood as he hisses and snarls like a wild beast. He pushes the woman aside and attacks Harker, throttling him until he passes out. He then inflicts an unseen wound upon the woman, causing her to scream in agony, and carries her limp body away into the shadows.

Harker awakes, and sees in the mirror that he has indeed been bitten – two small red punctures are livid in his throat. His final diary narration reveals that he is the victim of a terminal curse, and must act before nightfall if his mission is to be successful. He finally finds Dracula – blood on his lips – and the girl reposing in stone coffins. Perhaps unwisely, he decides to dispatch the girl first. He pulls a hammer and sharp wooden stake from his bag and – seen in silhouette – drives it into her body. A hideous scream rings out; our next view of the woman reveals her to have aged rapidly, she is now a grey and withered old crone. As Harker turns to Dracula, he finds to his horror that the Count has vanished. Then, Dracula reappears at the entrance to the crypt; the camera focuses in on his menacing presence, then cuts abruptly.

The next scene introduces the character of Professor Van Helsing, the vampire-hunter. Van Helsing arrives in the Klausenberg village inn in search of Harker, who it turns out was his friend and was working in league with him to destroy Count Dracula. The inn is decorated with garlic flowers, which shows Van Helsing that the locals are living in fear of Dracula; they deny all knowledge of Harker. Luckily, a kind serving wench slips him a copy of Harker's diary, and soon Van Helsing is driving by coach to Dracula's castle. As he arrives, a driverless funeral coach, pulled by black-plumed white horses and bearing a distinctive silver coffin, races from the castle gates and away into the night. Searching the castle, Van Helsing finds the corpse of the withered woman, a pool of blood around the stake in her heart, and then – in the next coffin – his friend Harker in repose. Realising that Harker has become a vampire, Van Helsing ruefully pulls his hammer and stake from his bag; fade-out.

We next see Van Helsing back home, breaking the news of Harker's death to Lucy, her brother Arthur, and Arthur's wife Mina. But sinister events soon start to unfold. That night we see Lucy throwing open her bedroom window – removing the silver crucifix from her neck – and then returning to bed in apparent anticipation. We then see a pair of livid bite-marks on her throat; cut to Van Helsing listening to a gramophone recording of his own voice detailing aspects of vampire lore – it is hear that we learn that "sunlight is fatal" to the vampire. The scene concludes with the admonition:

"Dracula must be found and destroyed".

Cut to Count Dracula, standing at Lucy's window. He enters, stoops over her, and then raises his cloak to mask the bite which we presume ensues.

Arthur and Mina puzzle over Lucy's growing illness, and consult Van Helsing. When he hears the word "anaemia", he is alerted to the truth. An examination of Lucy confirms his worst fears, and he prescribes garlic flowers, crosses and other anti-vampire paraphernalia. But that night Lucy awakes, stifling, and persuades her ignorant housekeeper to throw out the garlic and open the windows. She then lies back in almost sexual anticipation...cut to the next morning – her corpse is found, bloodless. Van Helsing reluctantly tells Arthur and Mina the truth, using Harker's diary as evidence.

In the next scene, a policeman arrives at Arthur's house – he has found little Tanya, the housekeeper's daughter, wandering and somewhat confused. She claims to have seen Lucy – alive and well! That night, Arthur checks the family crypt – sure enough, it is empty. Cut to scenes of Lucy once more talking to Tanya, luring her back to the crypt. Lucy has become a vampire, one of the undead. There she encounters Arthur and attempts to bite him. He thrusts out his big silver crucifix – it burns into her forehead and she is repulsed, fleeing back into the tomb. Van Helsing arrives, explaining that the cursing of Lucy is part of "Dracula's revenge". He stakes her through the heart – she screams, as if in relief, and is finally laid to rest.

Now Van Helsing and Arthur are sworn to exterminating the "unholy cult" of Dracula. Van Helsing realises that the silver coffin he saw being driven from DRacula's castle must have contained the Count himself, reposing in a bed of his own "native soil". They start a hunt for this coffin. Meanwhile, Mina receives a message, purporting to be from Arthur, to meet her at a specified address. In the next scene, Van Helsing learns from a bribed official that the mysterious coffin of Dracula was delivered to that very same address.

Mina arrives at the house, which turns out to be an undertaker's parlour full of coffins. The lid of one coffin begins to slowly slide back, revealing the presence of Count Dracula...

Next morning, Mina is not in bed at breakfast time. She then appears, looking pale and with her neck covered in a high fur collar, explaining she has been out for an early walk. Seemingly not suspicious at this, Arthur and Van Helsing set out to the undertaker's parlour in search of Dracula. They are too late – Dracula's coffin has vanished!

Back home, Arthur gives Mina a crucifix to wear; as she takes it, it sears her hand, causing her to faint. Alerted, Arthur and Van Helsing mount a nocturnal vigil outside the house to prevent further attacks by Count Dracula. Yet somehow he appears inside the house, unseen, and is soon in Mina's bedroom where he administers a sensual, sexualised bite. They find her the next morning, splashed in blood and near death. Arthur donates blood in a life-saving transfusion.

Later, Van Helsing realises that Dracula must have been in the house all along and, sure enough, finds the Count's coffin now housed in the cellar. He places a large silver cross in the coffin's soil to prevent Dracula returning, but it is too late – he has already vanished and taken Mina with him.

A frantic coach race now takes place, with Van Helsing pursuing Dracula and Mina back to his castle. As dawn approaches, Dracula tries to bury Mina alive, but is interrupted as Van Helsing arrives. The pair struggle inside the castle, with Dracula strangling Van Helsing to the point of unconsciousness. But the professor manages to break free and, realising that the sun is rising, tears down the great drapes which cover a castle window. Daylight streams in – the Count is transfixed by rays of light. Van Helsing fashions a makeshift cross from two silver candlesticks and uses it to hold Dracula powerless as the light pours over him. First Dracula's hands turn to dust, then the rest of him is reduced to crumbling bones. Mina's burn mark fades as the Count expires – the curse is lifted – and a chill morning wind sweeps through the castle, scattering Dracula's last remains and leaving only his signet ring as a reminder he ever existed. The end.

COMMENT

Christopher Lee's portrayal of Count Dracula quickly became regarded as so definitive that whenever people thought of Dracula, they envisioned Lee. His image, darkly virile and sexually-charged, lips glossed with bright blood, virtually revolutionised the global horror movie industry. Peter Cushing played the Count's perennial nemesis, the eminent vampirologist Dr. Van Helsing, armed with crucifixes, garlic flowers and the other paraphernalia of his rather specialised trade. Filmed in opulent colour, the film was far more explicit than the earlier Bela Lugosi version both in sexuality and bloodshed, with Dracula's female victims clearly enjoying rather than resisting his neck-biting advances. Van Helsing's comparison of vampirism to drug addiction underlines the theme of disease and delirium. It was largely this acknowledgement, and gradual development, of the sexual aspects inherent in the vampire myth which would make the

Hammer films in the genre so influential over the next fifteen years.

Jimmy Sangster's script presented a pared-down version of Stoker's novel, making some plot-changes along the way but basically preserving the highlights of the original. Amongst the major changes in the story is the role of Jonathan Harker, played by John Van Eyssen, who here appears as a vampire-hunter rather than a mere estate agent. His notorious encounter with the three female vampires is reduced to one. Other touches include the device of sunlight being fatal to the Count, and this, along with the other lore defined by Sangster in the script, became a guideline to vampire film-makers for years afterwards.

Directed by Terence Fisher, the film's most memorable moments include the scene in which Harker drives a stake through the heart of the beautiful young female vampire resting in her coffin, turning her into an aged, shrivelled hag before our eyes; Dracula's nocturnal visit to Lucy's bedroom; and the final showdown between the Count and Van Helsing in the former's castle. Typical of Fisher's `sadism' and `sexual disgust' are the shots where Lucy's unclean flesh is seared by a crucifix, while the inexorable invasion of both Mina's pristine home and her body by the vampire, while her protectors stand impotently in the grounds, illustrates perfectly his concept of the `beast within', the devil virus in the virgin flesh.

Dracula remains probably the finest example of the classic Hammer style, and combines the talents of the leading players and key production personnel who would go on to make that style world-famous. It has often been described as the best vampire film ever made, a fitting testament to its incredible initial impact.

FOOTNOTE

Christopher Lee was reluctant to portray Dracula again in a hurry for fear of type-casting, leaving Hammer with a dilemma in their desire for a follow-up to the hugely successful **Dracula**. In the end, **The Brides Of Dracula** (1960) retained the services of Peter Cushing as Van Helsing, but Hammer were forced to substitute David Peel as the chief vampire, Baron Meinster; Dracula does not in fact appear. Peel however made an interesting contrast to Lee; blond rather than swarthy, and somewhat sickly and effeminate compared to Lee's aggressive characterisation. Indeed, Meinster is kept locked up in his castle by his domineering mother (Marita Hunt), who prefers to select for herself the female victims to satisfy his vampiric urges. He also has his own nurse (Freda Jackson), a crazed and evil crone who coaxes the dead victims back to life from their graves at midnight. Meinster eventually burns to death in an old windmill whose sails have cast a paralysing cruciform shade upon the ground. The unusually well-etched female characters, emphasising the feminine mood of the film, and Terence Fisher's by now familiar use of sumptuous, saturated Technicolour, helped to make **The Brides Of Dracula** into one of the most attractive and admired films in the whole Hammer oeuvre.

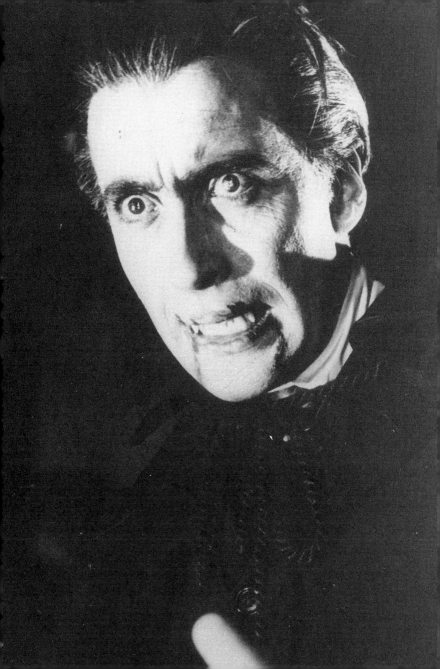

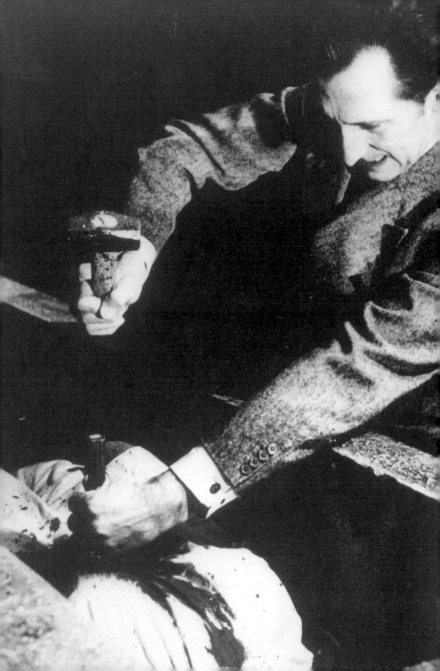

DRACULA,
PRINCE OF
DARKNESS

DRACULA, PRINCE OF DARKNESS (1966)

A Hammer-Seven Arts Production.

Dir: Terence Fisher. Sc: John Sansom, from an idea by John Elder [Anthony Hinds] based on the characters created by Bram Stoker. Ph: Michael Reed. Prod. des: Bernard Robinson. Art dir: Don Mingaye. Ed: James Needs, Chris Barnes. Mus: James Bernard. Prod: Anthony Nelson-Keys. Rel: Warner-Pathe (Britain), 20th Century-Fox (USA). 90 mins.

W: Christopher Lee (Dracula), Barbara Shelley (Helen), Andrew Keir (Father Sandor), Francis Matthews (Charles), Suzan Farmer (Diana), Charles Tingwell (Alan), Thorley Walters (Ludwig).

SYNOPSIS

Hammer's **Dracula, Prince Of Darkness** opens with a swirling optical effects as we are shown flashbacks to the last scenes of **Dracula**, in which the Count is turned to dust by Van Helsing's use of sunlight. The closing scenes feature a narration which speaks of the extermination of the "obscene cult of vampirism".

The film proper begins some 10 years later, with a woodland funeral procession in the Carpathian mountains. A dead girl, her pallid body borne on a stretcher, is about to be staked through the heart by a superstitious priest when a rifle shot rings out. Enter Father Sandor, an itinerant monk, who berates the priest for his "blasphemy", declaring that the threat of vampirism no longer exists in the region. Cut to a local inn, where we are introduced to four English travellers – Charles and his wife Diana, and Charles' elder brother Alan with his wife Helen. Right from the start, Helen is portrayed as an uptight, presumably frigid, scold. Enter Sandor, who warns them not to visit nearby Carlsbad – and above all, to avoid the castle there. Of course, they fail to heed this warning despite Helen's fears.

Next day, they are dumped some 2km from Carlsbad by the local coachman, who dreads nightfall. The castle looms nearby. As they debate their options a driverless coach approaches. Trying to steer it to Carlsbad, they are instead taken to the castle. Once they alight, the horses gallop away again. The castle door swings open...

Inside, they find a welcoming fire and a table set, mysteriously, for four guests. A search of the upper level reveals their luggage installed in two bedrooms. At this moment Helen is alarmed by the arrival of a shadowy figure. This turns out to be Klove, a manservant who explains that his master, one Count Dracula of "an old and distinguished family" who died "without issue – in the accepted sense of the term", is dead, but left instructions to welcome all strangers. Helen's forebodings increase, but the tired and hungry travellers decide to accept this hospitality. As they raise a toast to their absent host, a chill wind suddenly gusts through the castle, intensifying the undercurrent of dread.

As they retire, Helen repeats her assertion that the castle is an evil place. Alan tries to reassure her that things will be fine in the morning, but Helen's grim retort is simply: "For us there'll be no morning". This chilling premonition is quickly juxtaposed with an image of Klove snuffing out four candles – a stark visual portent of imminent extinction. Fade into night.

Helen awakes in the dead of night, sure she heard her name being called. Alan investigates and sees Klove, dragging a heavy trunk down the corridor. He follows and discovers a hidden stairway with leads to some kind of underground crypt. The centrepiece of this occult chamber is a huge stone sarcophagus – familiar from the first film – bearing the name DRACULA. Alan is suddenly stabbed in the back by Klove, and strung up by his feet over the tomb. Klove then fetches a funeral urn and pours ashes into the tomb. Then, in the film's most shocking sequence, he ritually slits Alan's throat and watches as gouts of vivid red blood fountain and froth over the ashes. A mist-shrouded, well-conceived body reintegration scene follows, as a human form seems to take shape within the tomb. Then a great peal of thunder breaks overhead, and a hand reaches over the edge – a hand bearing the familiar signet ring of Count Dracula. It seems that Klove – strangely absent from the first film – had nonetheless swept up the dusty remains of his master, and kept them for a decade, waiting for the right moment to bring the Count back from the dead.

Klove now summons Helen, who first sees her husband's butchered corpse and then the reanimated Dracula, who approaches and veils her with his cloak in familiar fashion...

Cut to the next day. Charles and Diana search the castle in vain for their missing relatives. Finally, Charles takes Diana to wait for him at the crossroads, before returning to the castle as dusk draws near. Scenes of him searching are intercut with Klove picking up Diana in his coach. Finally Charles finds the secret crypt, where Alan's body is stuffed in the trunk and Dracula reposes in his stone coffin. Night falls, and Dracula's eyes open. Klove shoves Diana into the castle and locks the door. Then Helen appears – she has undergone a complete physical transformation. Now clad in a low-cut white gown which accentuates her cleavage, she seems voluptuous and somehow wanton, the complete opposite of her former frigid self. As she approaches, Diana notices the two sharp fangs that gleam in Helen's mouth... Charles enters just as Helen moves to bite Diana. Helen then turns on Charles, but Dracula suddenly intervenes, throttling Charles. Seeing Diana's cross touch Helen and leave a searing burn mark in her flesh, Charles fashions a rudimentary cross from two swords and with this keeps the two vampires at bay as they flee, smashing Klove unconscious on the way. The coach soon overturns, but they are rescued by Father Sandor who gives them sanctuary in his monastery. There, he explains the nature of vampirism and Dracula, and also discusses ways to kill the Count – including the remark: "Running water will drown him".

The next night Klove draws up to the monastery in a coach bearing two coffins. He is forbidden entry, but allowed to camp in the grounds. Meanwhile, Sandor introduces Charles and Diana to Ludwig, their resident fly-eating lunatic. We soon find out that Ludwig is in fact a slave of Count Dracula, and that very night he beckons Dracula to enter the monastery (after Sandor has confidently explained that a vampire cannot enter any pace unless he is invited).

Diana is awoken by Helen, tapping at her window. Helen says she is cured now, but as soon as Diana opens up she lunges, biting her arm. Dracula then appears, but the vampires are driven away by the arrival of Sandor and several brothers. The monk cauterizes Diana's wound with a lamp.

They locate the vampires' coffins and place large silver crucifixes in them, so they may not return. Soon, Helen is captured, and dragged into a room. Spread-eagled on a table and held fast by several monks as if she is about to be gang-raped, Helen is staked through the heart by Sandor, who explains that her body is nothing but "a shell containing pure evil". Our last view of Helen shows her at peace.

Meanwhile Ludwig lures Helen to another room in the monastery, where she encounters Dracula. The Count appears to hypnotise her, forcing her to remove her crucifix. He then opens his shirt and draws his own blood using a sharp fingernail. As he draws Diana's head towards the blood as if to make her drink, he is interrupted and snatches her away, his coach soon heading back to the castle. Charles and Sandor, armed with a hunting rifle, pursue the coach on horseback. Taking a short cut, they manage to head the coach off at the crossroads. Klove is shot dead, but the horses bolt and career away towards castle Dracula. There, a coach wheel snags on the bridge, and Dracula's coffin is spilled onto the frozen moat. Diana is liberated, unharmed, from the other coffin.

Charles heads across the ice, armed with hammer and stake, to dispatch the Count. But it is too late – night falls – and Dracula springs from his coffin. As they struggle, Diana fires a random rifle shot. It ploughs into the ice, releasing running water. Sandor sees a way to kill Dracula, and starts shooting more bullets into the ice. As Charles flees, Dracula is isolated on a small plane of ice which soon cracks open, spilling him into the moat. The running water is fatal, and we see the vampire's death throes before he is submerged and vanishes. The end credits roll over a final, ghostly shot of his demonic face, eyes bulging, as he drowns beneath the ice.

COMMENT

After seven long years, Hammer fans got what they were craving – the return of Christopher Lee as Count Dracula. Terence Fisher once more directed, and **Dracula, Prince Of**

Darkness (1965) does not disappoint with its blend of Lee, lusting females, and visual poetry tempered with almost sadistic touches of violence. Peter Cushing, however, was conspicuous by his absence – he would not return to play Van Helsing again until 1972, in **Dracula AD 72**.

The strongest scenes in **Prince Of Darkness** are the act of throat-slitting by Klove, and the staking of the vampire Helen. The former is notable not only for excessive gore, but for its strong religious/anti-religious symbolism, which would recur throughout the series. The scene of Helen's eventual purification, with her convulsing form pinned down to a monastery table by priests so that she can be staked, is among the most effective in the cycle, a crystallisation of the clergy's libidinal terror; although Fisher's declared stance on the subjugation of wanton sexuality lends a distinct and uneasy ambivalence to the frame. Also is note is Lee's complete lack of dialogue, reduced from his minimal voicings of the first film to nothing but a series of snarls. This trend would be reversed in the next film in the series, **Dracula Has Risen From The Grave**.

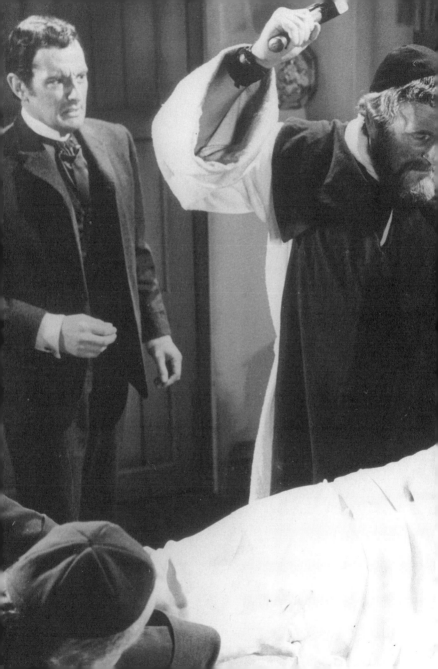

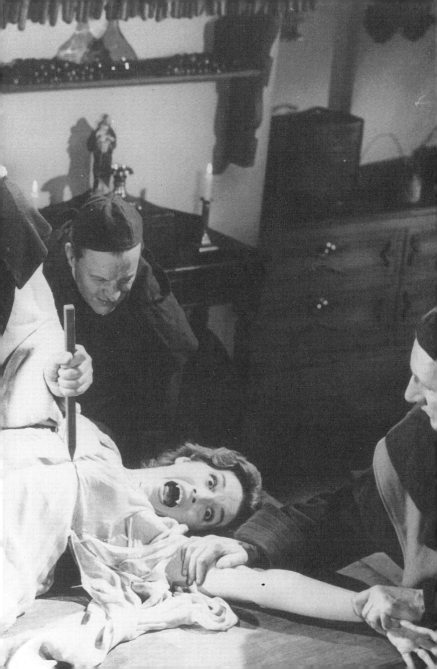

DRACULA
HAS RISEN FROM
THE GRAVE

DRACULA HAS RISEN FROM THE GRAVE (1968)

Dir: Freddie Francis. Sc: John Elder [Anthony Hinds] from the character created by Bram Stoker. Ph: Arthur Grant. Art dir: Bernard Robinson. Ed: James Needs, Spencer Reeve. Mus: James Bernard. Prod: Aida Young. Rel: Warner-Pathe (Britain), Warner Bros.-Seven Arts (USA). 92 mins. Technicolor.

W: Christopher Lee (Count Dracula), Rupert Davies (Monsignor), Veronica Carlson (Maria), Barbara Ewing (Zena), Barry Andrews (Paul), Ewan Hooper (Priest), Marion Mathie (Anna).

SYNOPSIS

Hammer's **Dracula Has Risen From The Grave** opens with a credits sequence of psychedelic swirls, followed by a shock flashback in which a young lad makes a terrifying discovery in a local church. As the lad goes to ring the church bell, he finds its rope coated in blood. He goes up into the belfry to investigate, and what he sees there strikes him mute with terror. The parish priest arrives and follows the trail of blood, which leads directly to the bell. As he draws near, a woman's corpse flops down from within the bell; her throat is marked by two savage, lacerated puncture marks, evidence of the predations of Count Dracula.

The next scene goes forward in time, and introduces us to the Monsignor; we learn that it is now 12 months since Dracula was destroyed in the icy running waters of the Carpathians, as seen in the previous film. When the Monsignor comes to this particular village, he finds the church still empty. In the local inn he is told by the villagefolk that although

Dracula is dead, they still shun the church because it lies within the evil shadow of the Count's castle. Outraged, the Monsignor declares he will go to castle Dracula at once, and perform an exorcism.

At dawn the next morning, he and the reluctant priest set up on their ascent of the fog-shrouded mountainside. As they near the castle the priest collapses, too fearful to continue. The Monsignor leaves him and carries on alone. He seals the gate of Dracula's castle with an enormous golden cross, and issues a prayer of exorcism as a violent thunderstorm breaks out and night falls prematurely. Back on the mountainside the priest, seeking shelter from the storm, slips and tumbles, cracking his head on a rock. By an obscene chance – or perhaps satanic design – he falls directly on the block of ice where Dracula's corpse has lain frozen for the last year, cracking it open. Blood from his head wound trickles into Dracula's mouth; the lips of blood quiver once more...

When the priest comes to, he sees the figure of Dracula, risen from his icy tomb, standing before him. Unable to resist, he falls under the vampire's power. While the Monsignor heads back to the village, Dracula and the priest return to the castle. Seeing the golden cross sealing his gates, Dracula recoils in horror. He asks the priest who has done this thing; the Count will have his revenge.

Next day the Monsignor returns to his home. Here we are introduced to his sister-in-law Anna, his niece Maria, and Maria's beau, Paul. At a dinner attended by these four, we learn the soon-to-be-crucial information that Paul is an atheist. This also gets him thrown out of the Monsignor's house, which followed by an inconsequential sequence in which he gets drunk and flirts with the local tart barmaid, Zena, until Maria comes to rescue him. Intercut with this banal action are dark scenes of the priest tipping a rotting corpse from its coffin so that the Count may lie in it, and then Dracula's funeral coach, pulled by black-plumed horses, speeding through the night towards the Monsignor's home town. By the time Paul returns from the abortive dinner, the coach is tied up outside his local inn.

As Zena walks home later that night, she is followed through the woods by the coach. As she tries to flee, she suddenly comes face to face with Dracula. As his eyes meet hers she seems to surrender, her bodice barely concealing her ample breasts, and willingly succumbs to his bite.

Next morning Zena is seen nervously eyeing the two livid punctures on her throat. At this point the priest enters the inn, and takes the spare upstairs room. That evening the priest slips down into the cellar bakery, and opens up a door concealed behind sacks of grain. It leads to a strange, crypt-like chamber where the coffin containing Count Dracula is resting. The coffin lid crashes open; Dracula stands in the shadows. Later on, the priest summons Zena to this chamber; She seems pleassed to see the Count, but he spurns her proffered throat and instead instructs her to fetch him Maria; when she cavils, he slaps her violently to the floor. Zena carries out his orders, and when she has lured Maria to the cellar she pulls a sack over her head then bundles her into the Count's makeshift crypt. Dracula begins to hypnotise Maria, but Paul interrupts by making noise next door and the spell is – for now – broken. Dracula punishes Zena for this – "you have failed me" – administering a fatal bite. The priest disposes of Zena's body by shoving it into the fiery ovens. Paul then makes a bad mistake – he asks the priest to visit Maria and hand her a note.

That night, it is Dracula who invades Maria's room, invited in by proxy, where he seduces her and administers his sensual, deadly bite.

Next day the Monsignor finds Maria pale and ill. Suspicious, he looks for, and finds, the tell-tale bite marks of a vampire's attack. He makes sure Maria's windows are closed that night, but unfortunately does not know enough about vampire lore to take other, more effective, precautions. That night Dracula enters again; he is interrupted by the Monsignor and flees over the rooftops, pursued by the Monsignor who is then knocked senseless by the priest.

The next day, dying from his injuries, the Monsignor sends for Paul and instructs him to keep vigil over Maria, giving him some books on vampire lore. Paul carries out the recommended precautions – assisted by the priest.

Night falls. The priest, under Dracula's sway, knocks Paul unconscious and starts to remove the garlic flowers and other talismans from around Maria's bed. As he hesitates over touching her crucifix Paul comes to, grabs him and forces him to lead him to Dracula's lair. Paul drives a huge wooden stake through Dracula's heart but – because of his atheism – is unable to recite a requisite prayer. This enables Dracula to pull out the stake, in a fountain of gushing blood, and escape death once again. The Count once more heads out over the rooftops, where he trysts with the somnambulistic Maria and bears her away in his coach; "now my revenge is complete".

As Dracula's coach heads towards his castle, Paul pursues on horseback. He stops at the village inn for directions and is finally guided by the mute bell-ringer. Meanwhile Dracula's coach pulls up in a moonlit glade; the Count glides through the forest, followed by the bare-footed Maria; finally he carries her up to the very threshold of his castle, as if they are newly-weds from Hell. Here, she must remove the huge golden cross that bars their way. Maria manages to heave the cross over the parapet; it falls far below and lands upright, embedded in the soil.

At this point Paul arrives, and hurls himself upon Dracula. After a brief struggle, The vampire Count slips and himself plunges over the stone rampart, impaling himself on the pointed gold cross as he lands. As Dracula struggles, the priest is liberated from his thrall and, finally, says the necessary prayers. Dracula, agonized tears of blood streaming from his eyes, finally slumps back in death. The last shot in the film is of the blood-drenched cross and Dracula's cloak, now empty of its disintegrating occupant, sliding to the ground.

COMMENT

Freddie Francis, whose skills as a brilliant cinematographer are hinted at by the filter effects which herald Dracula's appearances, is nonetheless a lesser director than Terence Fisher. The dualities and tensions of the previous two **Dracula** films are replaced by a much more banal schema, sadism by brutality. Yet the film still has evocative moments – in particular, the moonlight walk of Maria and her dark captor. The sexuality of vampirism is made even more explicit than before, with Dracula almost making love to his willing female victims as he prepares to drain their blood. Notable for its extraordinarily religious orientation, the film also pointed the way for the more Satanic element Hammer would introduce in the later **Dracula** films. It also restored some dialogue – albeit monosyllabic – to the character of Count Dracula.

TASTE
THE BLOOD
OF DRACULA

TASTE THE BLOOD OF DRACULA (1970)

Dir: Peter Sasdy. Sc: John Elder [Anthony Hinds] based on the character created by Bram Stoker. Ph: Arthur Grant. Art dir: Scott MacGregor. Ed: Chris Barnes. Mus: James Bernard. Prod: Aida Young. Rel: Warner-Pathe (Britain), Warner Bros.-Seven Arts (USA). 95 mins. Technicolor.

W: Christopher Lee (Count Dracula), Geoffrey Keen (William Hargood), Gwen Watford (Martha Hargood), Linda Hayden (Alice Hargood), Peter Sallis (Samuel Paxton), John Carson (Secker), Roy Kinnear (Antiques Dealer), Isla Blair (Lucy), Ralph Bates (Courtley).

SYNOPSIS

Hammer's **Taste The Blood Of Dracula** opens with the usual ominous musical strains, as a coach hurtles through a forest in the Carpathians. On board is an English antiques dealer , who is suddenly hurled from the carriage by a retarded fellow passenger. When he comes to, it is night. He hears terrible screams, and investigates. What he finds is the sight of Count Dracula, impaled on a giant golden cross and bleeding from every orifice, as last seen in the dying moments of the previous film. As Dracula expires, the dealer approaches his remains and scoops up the Count's clasp, cloak and powdered blood.

Cut to England, a church service, where we are introduced to three upper middle class gentlemen – Hargood, Paxton and Secker – and their various offspring. It soon transpires that these outwardly religious, puritanical patriarchs are in fact dissolute roués who, under the guise of East End charity work, make monthly visits to a Hellfire Club-style brothel. On their latest visit they are rudely interrupted by Courtley, a young rake renowned for his excesses and Satanic connections. Intrigued, the three men take him for dinner, anxious to learn of new and greater debauches. Courtley suggests nothing less than selling their souls to the Devil – a proposal they accept with varying degrees of enthusiasm.

Next, they must purchase the necessary relics for a Satanic ritual, and Courtley takes them to the very same antiques dealer who we saw at the film's opening. For the sum of 1,000 guineas, they are offered the last physical remnants of "the Master" – the clasp, cloak and dried blood of Count Dracula. This sequence is intercut with scenes of a secret love tryst between Hargood's daughter, Alice, and Paxton's son Paul.

Cut to the night of the ceremony. They travel by coach to an old church in the countryside, where Courtley awaits them in the crypt. Here, he has erected a Satanic altar lit by black candles. Courtley first pours a measure of Dracula's blood into three crystal goblets, then adds drops of his own freshly-drawn blood. As he does, the Count's powdered blood is rehydrated and wells to the brim of each glass, and thunder wells in the background. Now Courtley exhorts each of them to drink of the blood – but none of them can bear to do so. Enraged, Courtley drinks down a chalice himself – and promptly dies in agony, helped by a few kicks from the horrified men. They flee. Soon Courtley's body is covered in a dust which is whipped in by a chill wind; then the dust cracks open to reveal the red-eyed form of Count Dracula. Once more, the vampire king is risen from the dead. At once, he swears revenge on the three gentlemen: "They have destroyed my servant – they will be destroyed".

Cut to the next day. Scenes of the three gentlemen, who are badly shaken but confident they have gotten away with murder. We also see Alice sneaking out to go to a party with Paul, against her father's orders, and Count Dracula emerging from a tomb – whose former occupant, a withered corpse, he has ejected onto the floor – and exit into the night.

As Alice returns from the party she is caught by her drunken father, who threatens to whip her. As she flees into the garden, she is accosted by Dracula, who hypnotises her and is about to bite her when interrupted by her father. Yet she is still under his sway, and at his silent bidding she caves in her father's head with a shovel. "The first."

Next day, Hargood is found dead, and Alice is missing. And that night, Dracula stalks his second victim – Paxton. Still under his power, Alice lures Paxton's daughter, Lucy. into a coach which takes them at terrifying sped to the old church crypt. Dracula advances upon her, she resists briefly but then falls under his spell and is bitten through the throat by the red-eyed vampire.

Soon, fearing that Hargood was somehow killed by Courtley, Paxton and Secker go back to the crypt in search of the young rake's body. It is gone. Frantic, they decide to check a tomb which appears to have been opened – and find Lucy lying within. Secker, who seems to have knowledge of vampirism, realises that she is one of the undead. He makes to stake her through the heart, but is shot in the arm by Paxton and staggers out to collapse in the graveyard. Night falls. Paxton, who has kept a grieving vigil by his daughter's side, finally accepts that he must stake her to release her from the curse. But she wakes just in time, as Alice and Dracula enter the crypt. Under the Count's bidding, Alice holds Paxton down while Lucy drives the stake through her father's heart. "The second."

Secker comes to the next morning, sees the coffin empty, and returns home. That evening, his son, Jeremy, is accosted by Lucy (his sweetheart). As Dracula watches, Lucy bites Jeremy as he bends to kiss her. Now one of the vengeful undead, Jeremy goes to his father's study and stabs him through the stomach, killing him. "The third."

It appears that Dracula has yet to bite Alice. Now she has fulfilled her purpose, he advances on her to administer the curse of the undead. Just then a cock crows, signalling daybreak. Dracula halts, turns and flees back to his coffin.

Later that day, Paul reads a last letter written by Secker, in which Secker warns him of Dracula, and explains how the vampire must be destroyed. This is intercut with a scene of Dracula, reposing in his tomb with the stone lid askew, and Alice sleeping on top of the lid, as if embracing her new father/lover.

Early next day Paul goes to the old church. Here he finds the body of Lucy, fatally bitten. He bars closed the crypt door with a large cross then sets about making the altar holy again, lighting white candles and draping it with a white altar cloth. He calls for Alice – and is assailed by the cacophony of night as she approaches with Count Dracula. Paul repels Dracula with a crucifix, but Alice grabs his arm and Dracula escapes, only to be trapped by the cross which bars the crypt door. Alice is freed from Dracula's spell and flees as the enraged Count hurls things at them. Climbing up over the altar, Dracula is suddenly confronted by a holy cross in a stained glass window. He angrily smashes the window and starts to climb through, but finds that he has penetrated the church next door, which is a veritable forest of white candles, crosses and other Christian paraphernalia. Transfixed by this religious onslaught, he falls and crashes onto the sacred altar where he perishes, apparently destroyed by a surfeit of holiness. The end credits roll over a garish red image of his liquefied body.

COMMENT

New directorial talent was interestingly in evidence when TV director Peter Sasdy was given control over **Taste The Blood Of Dracula**. Sasdy produces some stunning images, and revels in the film's Satanic undertones. Despite remarking in 1969 that "I feel I would almost have to be forced into doing it for a fourth time", Christopher Lee again returned to play the Count.

The film uses the now-familiar plot device of Dracula taking revenge on his male enemies by corrupting and/or killing the wives/girlfriends/daughters most dear to them. The Count's dialogue remains minimal, but effective.

Dracula's position as `anti-Christ' is emphasised by the Satanic rites which recall him to life, and also in his polar opposition to the notion of the nuclear family – the daughters are turned into castrating angels who carry out the vampire's revenge upon their patriarchal oppressors. From now on, a black mass or other mark of fealty to Satan would nearly always figure in the proceedings.

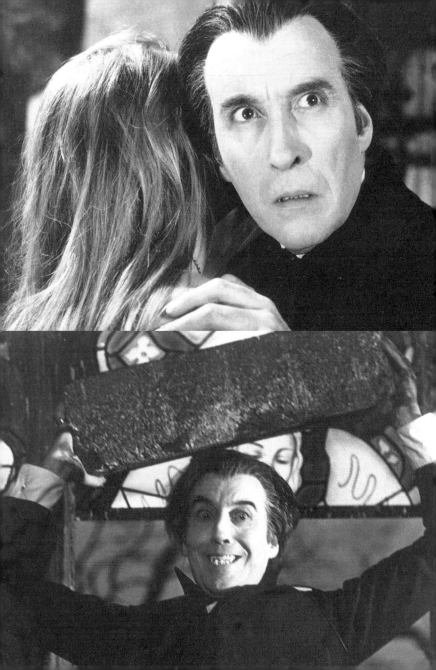

The **TERRIFYING** Lover—
who died – yet lived!

Universal-International presents A Hammer Film Production

PETER CUSHING in

DRACULA

(Cert. X) Adults only

MICHAEL GOUGH
with MELISSA STRIBLING
with CHRISTOPHER LEE as Dracula

In Eastman Colour processed by Technicolor

Screenplay by JIMMY SANGSTER   Associate Producer ANTHONY NELSON-KEYS
Produced by ANTHONY HINDS   Directed by TERENCE FISHER
Executive Producer MICHAEL CARRERAS

Distributed by Rank Film Distributors Ltd.

DON'T DARE SEE IT ALONE!

The chill of the tomb won't leave
your blood for hours...after you
come face-to-face with **DRACULA!**

WHO WILL BE HIS BRIDE TONIGHT?

ALL NEW!

HORROR OF DRACULA

in Brilliant **TECHNICOLOR!**

starring PETER CUSHING · also starring MICHAEL GOUGH and MELISSA STRIBLING with CHRISTOPHER LEE as DRACULA

Universal Film, Inc. *présente*

LE CAUCHEMAR DE DRACULA

(HORROR OF DRACULA)

AVEC PETER CUSHING · MICHAEL GOUGH ET MELISSA STRIBLING
ET CHRISTOPHER LEE DANS LE RÔLE DE DRACULA
UNE PRODUCTION HAMMER FILM EN COULEURS · MISE EN SCÈNE TERENCE FISHER

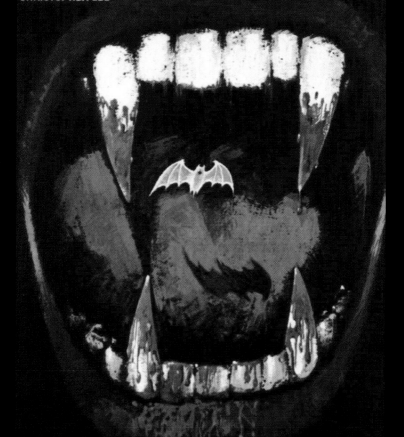

DRACULA PRINCIPE DE LAS TINIEBLAS

CHRISTOPHER LEE

BARBARA SHELLEY · ANDREW KEIR

PRODUCIDA POR ANTHONY NELSON KEYS · DIRIGIDA POR TERENCE FISHER · GUION DE JOHN SANSOM · COLOR

DRACULA PRINCE OF DARKNESS

DRACULA HAS RISEN FROM THE GRAVE

CHRISTOPHER LEE

PERT DAVIES · VERONICA CARLSON · BARBARA EWING · BARRY ANDREWS · EWAN HOOP

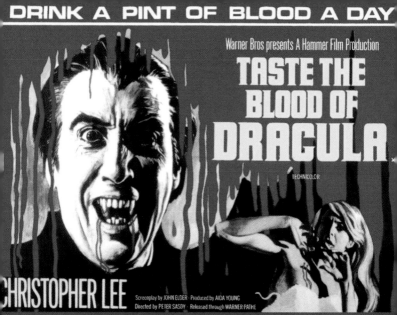

Warner Bros presents A Hammer Film Production

TASTE THE BLOOD OF DRACULA

TECHNICOLOR

CHRISTOPHER LEE

Screenplay by JOHN ELDER · Produced by AIDA YOUNG
Directed by PETER SASDY · Released through WARNER-PATHE

COLFILM PRODUCTIONS LTD present A HAMMER PRODUCTION

SCARS OF DRACULA

starring CHRISTOPHER LEE
with DENNIS WATERMAN · JENNY HANLEY · CHRISTOPHER MATTHEWS

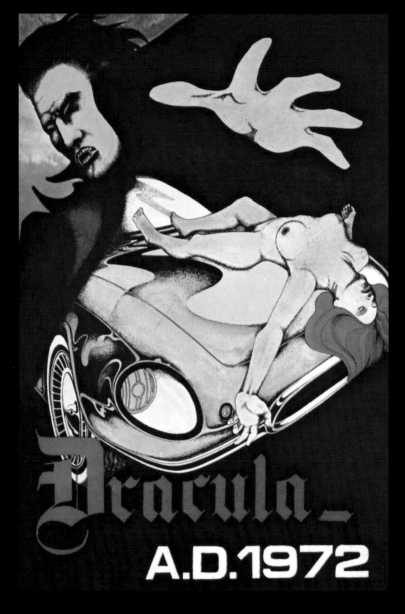

THIS IS A
HAMMER
FILM

DRACULA
73

CHRISTOPHER LEE · PETER CUSHING

STEPHANIE BEACHAM · CHRISTOPHER NEAME · MICHAEL COLES

NEW FROM HAMMER!

THE TIME: NOW
THE PLACE: KINGS ROAD, CHELSEA
THE KILLER: COUNT DRACULA

DRACULA
A.D. 1972

Warner Bros a Warner Communications Company Presents A Hammer Production Starring
CHRISTOPHER LEE · PETER CUSHING
And Starring STEPHANIE BEACHAM · CHRISTOPHER NEAME
MICHAEL COLES

I SATANICI RITI DI DRACULA

(THE SATANIC RITES OF DRACULA)

UNA PRODUZIONE HAMMER FILM CON **CHRISTOPHER LEE** **PETER CUSHING** **MICHAEL COLES**

THE SCARS
OF DRACULA

THE SCARS OF DRACULA (1970)

Dir: Roy Ward Baker. Sc: John Elder [Anthony Hinds] from the char-
acter created by Bram Stoker. Ph: Moray Grant. Art dir: Scott
MacGregor. Ed: James Needs. Mus: James Bernard. Prod: Aida
Young. Rel: MGM-EMI (Britain). 96 mins. Technicolor.
W: Christopher Lee (Count Dracula), Dennis Waterman (Simon),
Jenny Hanley (Sarah Framsen), Christopher Matthews (Paul), Patrick
Troughton (Klove), Michael Gwynn (Priest).

SYNOPSIS

Hammer's **The Scars Of Dracula** opens with a night-time
view of a castle high in the Carpathian mountains. Here we see
the remains of Count Dracula, as last glimpsed at the end of
the previous film – they have somehow been transported from
England, it seems. A huge vampire bat hovers over the
remains, and fresh blood – evidently human – drips from its
fangs and onto the ashes below. Within seconds, Count Dracula
is risen from the dead.

Cut to a daylight shot of a peasant bearing a young
woman's body across the fields. As he carries her into the
village inn, we see that her throat has been savagely bitten
through. Outraged, the menfolk of the village decide that they
must act now, to stop this evil once and for all. Locking up their
women in the sanctuary of the church, and accompanied by the
village priest, they storm up to Dracula's castle, bursting past
the Count's servant, Klove – a different Klove to the one seen
in **Dracula, Prince Of Darkness** – and set fire to the castle.
Meanwhile, Dracula reposes high in his unreachable chamber.

His pet bat hovers overhead; the two appear to be communing.

The villagers finally leave, satisfied that the blazing fire will consume Dracula. When they get back to the church, vampire bats swarm out. Inside, a scene of bloody horror and carnage – all their women have been killed by the bats, faces and bodies torn to shreds, eyeballs ripped out. The church resembles a slaughterhouse, and this is certainly the most profane and gory scene in the series to date. Dracula has taken immediate and devastating revenge for the attack on his castle.

Cut to a birthday party in Kleinenberg. Here we meet Simon and Sarah, the young lovers and protagonists of the film. Sarah is wondering where paul, Simon's elder brother, has got to. We soon see that he is in bed with the burgomaster's daughter. When he hurries away to get to Sarah's party, the girl cries rape and Paul is pursued by soldiers. This sequence affords the first glimpse of female nudity (from the rear) in the series to date. Fleeing into the woods, Paul comes to the village inn, but after the barmaid lets him in, he is sent packing by the landlord. Back in the forest he finds an empty coach, climbs in and falls asleep. But the coach belongs to Count Dracula; Klove, hunting for deer, soon returns and speeds off to the castle.

Paul awakes in the ruins of castle Dracula. A vampire bat swoops at him, then he sees Tanya, a voluptuous young woman dressed in purple. Tanya invites him into the castle, where he meets Dracula. He is welcomed; while Klove shows Paul to his room, Tanya and Dracula "make love" in their own special way, the Count biting her throat as she sighs in ecstasy. But later that night, Tanya comes to Paul's room. She tells him she is a prisoner, and begs him to help her – and to make love to her. Paul obliges. Near dawn, Tanya awakes and eyes Paul's exposed throat greedily. Just then Dracula bursts in, enraged, and butchers her with a dagger. Before he can turn on Paul, the cock crows heralding daybreak, and the Count vanishes.

Paul tries to escape. Outside his window is a sheer drop into the ravines below. He knots together drapes from the bed, and manages to climb down to an open window. Here he finds a coffin, its nameplate engraved with the single word DRACULA. Meanwhile, Klove sets to dismembering and disposing of Tanya's body. Finding a framed photo of Sarah which Paul has left behind (it was a birthday present for her), the deformed servant seems to fall in love with her image.

Cut to the forest, where Simon and Sarah are wandering in search of Paul. They reach the small village, but at the inn they are told nothing until the kind barmaid confirms that Paul was there the day before, and had headed off to the castle. They follow after him – watched by a vampire bat. As they near the castle, we see Klove, still gloating over Sarah's photo. In the courtyard they are attacked by a bat, and driven inside. Dracula welcomes them. When Sarah faints, the Count picks her up and carries her to a bedroom. Klove makes Paul a bed downstairs.

Later that night, Dracula enters Sarah's room, watching her as she sleeps. He bends over to bite her, but is repelled by the crucifix around her neck. Klove is summoned and ordered to remove the offending object. But he recognises Sarah – the girl whose image he has fallen in love with – and refuses, leaving Dracula seething with fury.

Next morning finds Simon and Sarah both unscathed. While Sarah has breakfast, Simon investigates the castle. He finds Klove's room. Klove – whose back bears the livid welts and lacerations of Dracula's punishment – warns them to leave at once. They flee and take Dracula's coach, driving back to the village inn. Once more they are rebuffed, but the village priest comes to their aid, giving them sanctuary in his desecrated church. Here, he explains the nature of Dracula, and what must be done to destroy him. Back at the castle, we see Dracula punishing Klove by branding his back with a white-hot sword.

That night the barmaid quits in disgust at the men's cowardice, and sets off through the woods. Dracula dispatches Klove to abduct her and bring her back to the castle. Dracula hypnotises her and feasts on her throat, with eyes burning red and lips of blood.

Next day Simon and the priest set off to castle Dracula, bent on destroying the vampire Count. The priest's courage falters; Simon sends him back to guard Sarah, and carries on alone. At the castle he forces Klove to show him where Paul is being kept. He uses a rope to climb down into Dracula's secret chamber, and finds the Count in reposes. As he is about the stake him through the heart, Dracula's eyes seem to burn red through his closed eyelids, sending Simon into a faint. Meanwhile, a huge vampire bat enters the village church and attacks the priest, shredding his face and killing him. Sarah flees in terror into the forest.

Simon comes to after nightfall. Dracula is gone, and Simon then finds Paul's body, butchered and hung up impaled on a meathook. Enter Dracula, seeking Sarah's whereabouts. Just then his bat enters, communing with the Count, who learns that she is in fact on her way to the castle. Dracula exits, and we see him walk up the castle wall and into the room above.

As Sarah reaches the castle, Klove lunges at her but Dracula intervenes, hypnotising her. Repelled by her crucifix once more, he summons his vampire bat to tear it from her neck. The bat obeys, affording a lingering erotic close-up of her swelling, barely-covered breasts streaked with fresh blood. Meanwhile Klove has thrown a rope to Paul, allowing him to escape from Dracula's chamber. The love-sick servant then attacks his master with a dagger in Sarah's defence, and is hurled over the castle parapet to his death below. Simon arrives, rips out a metal pole from the wall and launches it at Dracula. It penetrates the Count's chest but apparently misses his heart. He rips it out and prepares to throw it back at Simon with deadly force. Just then a bolt of lightning crashes down and strikes the pole, violently electrocuting Dracula who bursts into flames. As he burns, screaming, we see a close-up of his hideously blistering face before he too topples from the parapet and plunges, a human torch, to extinction. The end.

COMMENT

The Scars Of Dracula is something of a one-off in the series, which had reached a natural conclusion of sorts in **Taste The Blood Of Dracula**. It features more sex, gore and overt violence than before (though still tame by today's standards). Lee's portrayal of the Count reaches its physical peak in this film; he is afforded more screen-time, much more dialogue, and looks sublime with dead white pallor and red contact-lenses, indulging in some spectacular – if out of character – moments of sadistic violence. Another notable difference is the perfunctory resurrection scene – in all the other films in the series, Dracula's resurrection is treated with great care and ingenuity, and comes after a lengthy build-up.

Not all of the film's innovations are a success, however – the scenes when Dracula communes with his very fake-looking bat are verging on the ridiculous. This was also the last time Dracula would operate in his native country; with the next two films in the series, he was thrust back to England, and hauled screaming into the 20th Century.

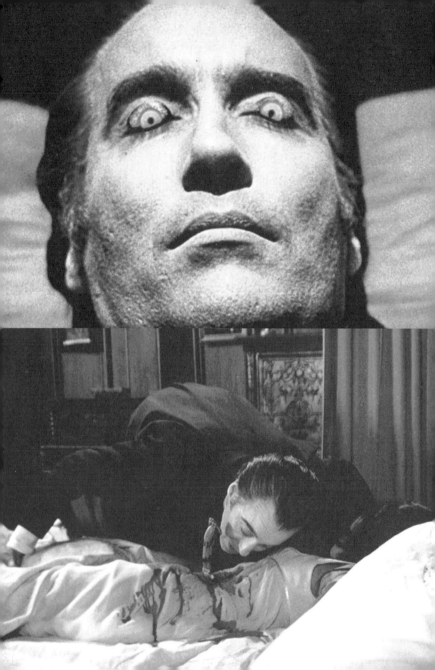

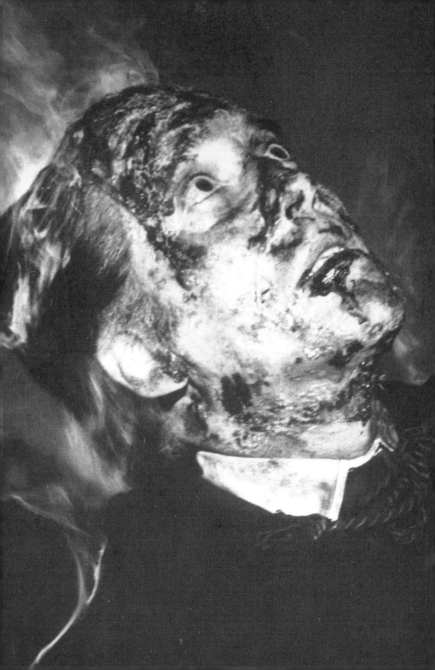

DRACULA
AD 72

DRACULA AD 72 (1972)

Dir: Alan Gibson. Sc: Don Houghton. Ph: Dick Bush. Prod. des: Don Mingaye. Ed: James Needs. Mus: Michael Vickers. Prod: Josephine Douglas. Rel: Warner Bros. (Britain: through Columbia-Warner). 97 mins Eastman Colour.

W: Christopher Lee (Count Dracula), Peter Cushing (Prof. Van Helsing), Stephanie Beacham (Jessica Van Helsing), Michael Coles (Inspector), Christopher Neame (Johnny Alucard), William Ellis (Joe Mitchum), Marsha Hunt (Gaynor), Janet Key (Anna), Philip Miller (Bob), Michael Kitchen (Greg).

SYNOPSIS

Hammer's **Dracula AD 72** opens with a horse-drawn carriage hurtling through the night, pursued at distance by a man on horseback. A narration informs us that the place is Hyde Park, London, the year 1872; we are about to witness the final confrontation between Lawrence Van Helsing and his arch enemy, the "demon Dracula" (this despite the fact that the encounter between the two in the first film, **Dracula**, took place in 1885). Suddenly the coach crashes and both men are hurled out. When Van Helsing gets up, he sees that Count Dracula has been impaled by a wooden wheel spoke. Falling on the vampire, he drives it home, through the heart, killing him. Van Helsing is also fatally injured, however, and collapses and dies soon afterward. When the horseman arrives, it transpires he is a disciple of Dracula who gathers up the Count's signet ring and a phial of his ashes.

Cut to the funeral of Van Helsing. Just beyond the

cemetery, in unhallowed ground, we see Dracula's disciple bury some of his master's ashes in an unmarked grave, securing them in the earth with a wooden stake. Cut to 1972 – an age of motorway fastlanes, trains, planes and industrial cranes, announced by a strident modern jazz soundtrack. Cut to a party in Chelsea, where a rock band plays in an extended sequence and we are introduced to Johnny Alucard and his gang – a group of young, trendy types that includes one Jessica Van Helsing.

We next see the gang in the Cavern, the trendy café bar they frequent, discussing their hunger for new kicks. Johnny has a suggestion – a "date with the Devil". The group agree to try a black mass.

Jessica returns home, where we meet her grandfather, Lorrimar Van Helsing – a demonologist and the grandson of Lawrence Van Helsing.

That night – the "feast of Belphegor" – Johnny assembles his gang in an unhallowed church near Chelsea. We soon learn that this is the very same church where Lawrence Van Helsing was buried, one hundred years ago to the day. As Johnny prepares for the ritual, we see that he has in his possession the ring and ashes of Count Dracula. Bidding the group to sit in a black magic circle, he plays a pagan drum track on his tape recorder and then begins the rites, invoking all the demons of Hell and including the name of Count Dracula on that infernal roll call. As the ritual progresses, a chill wind whips up and, outside, smoke seeps from the earth where Dracula's ashes were also interred a century before. Johnny bids one of the girls, Laura, to lie on the Satanic altar, holding a goblet. Johnny pours Dracula's ashes into the goblet then slashes his arm and drips his blood into it. As the goblet wells over with gore, the rest of the gang are freaked out and flee in terror. Johnny goes to the graveyard and pulls out the stake planted there by his own ancestor; more smoke rushes out, and in a matter of seconds Count Dracula stands before him, once more made flesh. The vampire overlord wastes no time in claiming Laura as his first victim, biting through her neck and gorging on her blood as Johnny watches his new master.

Next day the group assemble at the Cavern, but Laura is missing. Johnny says she went to Ramsgate, and that last night's ritual was just a hoax, but Jessica is unconvinced. This is intercut with a shot of Laura's corpse, mutilated and drained of blood, being discovered by a group of boys playing near the desecrated church.

A police investigation commences. Meanwhile Johnny seduces and dopes another female member of the group, Gaynor, and takes her to Dracula. He bites and kills her, but is dissatisfied; Jessica is the one he wants. Johnny begs his master for the gift of immortality; when we next see him, stalking a girl at night, he bears a telltale bite on his neck, and the fangs of the undead.

The police, linking dead Laura to Jessica, speak to her and her grandfather. Van Helsing's ears prick up when he hears that Laura was exsanguinated; and when Jessica tells him about Johnny Alucard, he quickly realises that the young man's name is DRACULA spelled backwards. He places a crucifix around Jessica's neck, and begins to arm himself with weapons that may destroy a vampire – holy water, a silver dagger, a bible – then tries to explain the curse of Dracula to the baffled police.

That night Bob, Jessica's boyfriend, finds Johnny at

the Cavern after hours. Later he calls on Jessica and takes her back there, ostensibly to speak to the police. But when they arrive, only Johnny is waiting there; Bob has also become one of the undead. He bears his fangs and moves to bite Jessica, but is prevented by Johnny – "she belongs to the master".

Van Helsing discovers Jessica is missing and tracks her to the Cavern, but too late. Outside he meets another of the group, Anna, who tells him Alucard's address. He rushes there just as Johnny is preparing to leave, and confronts him. It is nearing dawn, and Johnny grows agitated. He attacks Van Helsing, who throws a bible into Johnny's makeshift coffin to stop him hiding there as daylight starts to seep into the room. Johnny stabs Van Helsing but the professor, using light reflected from a mirror, drives the vampire back into the bathroom. He slips, falls into the bath and accidentally activates the shower. Clear running water drowns the blistered vampire.

Van Helsing heads to the unhallowed church, where he first finds Bob's bloodless corpse, and then his granddaughter, who is lying in Dracula's spell. He places another cross around her neck, then passes the hours before nightfall preparing a boobytrap – a grave filled with razor sharp stakes – in the church grounds.

Night falls. Dracula appears and approaches his sleeping bride. She wakes, he grabs the crucifix – burning his hand – and stoops to administer his fatal bite. Van Helsing interrupts and the two are soon engaged in a life-or-death struggle. Van Helsing stabs Dracula with his silver knife, and the Count plunges to the church floor. But Jessica, still under his spell, removes the blade before it can be fatal. Dracula pursues Van Helsing into the cemetery; the professor hurls the holy water into his face and the vampire loses his footing, slips and falls into the spiked grave, impaling himself on the stakes. To finish him off, Van Helsing drives a shovel through Dracula's back; the vampire king is killed, and disintegrates once more, his skull oozing putrid flesh.

The words REST IN FINAL PEACE – Lawrence Van Helsing's epitaph – appear across the screen. The end.

COMMENT

Variously known as "Dracula Today" and even "Dracula Chelsea '72" during production, **Dracula AD 72** was later described by Michael Carreras as "a mistake". "There is only one Dracula, and his period must never be changed," was Christopher Lee's accurate summation of the project. Nonetheless, the film had some positive points. For one, it marked the long-awaited return of Peter Cushing to the series, in his role as Van Helsing.

The Satanic mass leading to the Count's resurrection was the best realised and most dramatic yet, and also marked Dracula's elevation to the very ranks of the demons of Hell. Dracula's dispatch was also the most prolonged, violent and sadistic yet filmed, emphasising the personal vendetta between him and Van Helsing; this time the vampire was stabbed, sustained a fall onto stone, was seared with holy water, impaled by not the usual one but by dozens of stakes, and finally virtually cut in half with a shovel.

Despite rehashing plot devices and themes from nearly all of the previous films in the series, **Dracula AD 72** at least signalled a willingness to experiment with formula by Hammer and, although it now appears hopelessly dated, it can still be viewed as a partial success, at least.

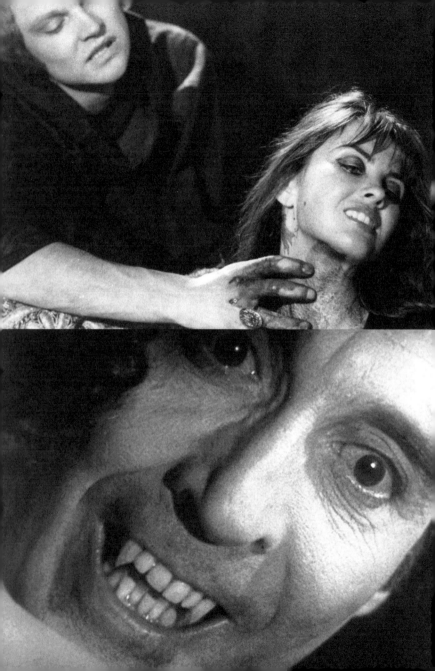

DAD—43

THE
SATANIC RITES
OF DRACULA

THE SATANIC RITES OF DRACULA (1973)

(US: **Count Dracula And His Vampire Bride** [1978])

Dir: Alan Gibson. Sc: Don Houghton. Ph: Brian Probyn. Art dir: Lionel
Couch. Ed: Christopher Barnes. Prod: Roy Skeggs. Rel: Warner Bros.
(Britain: through Columbia-Warner). Colour.

W: Christopher Lee (Count Dracula), Peter Cushing (Van Helsing),
William Franklyn (Torrence), Michael Coles (Inspector Murray), Joanna
Lumley (Jessica), Freddie Jones (Prof. Keeley), Barbara Yu Ling (Chin
Yang), Valerie Ost (Jane), Richard Vernon (Col. Mathews).

SYNOPSIS

Hammer's **The Satanic Rites Of Dracula** opens with night
shots of modern London. Cut to a Satanic mass attended by
hooded figures with foreheads daubed in red inverted crosses;
on the altar a nude girl (the first glimpse of full-frontal nudity
in the series). All the demons of Hell are invoked. We see that
the black mass is being held in a country house guarded by
thugs bizarrely dressed in uniform fur-trimmed waistcoats.
Upstairs a prisoner, though badly beaten, manages to escape.
As the alarm goes off he is pursued by thugs on motorbikes,
but they are shot and killed by figures in a getaway car beyond
the perimeter.

Next day the man – evidently some kind of
government agent – describes the obscene rituals which he
observed in the house. As he describes them, we are shown
them – the slaughter of a cockrel followed by a human
sacrifice, as the nude girl on the altar is stabbed through the
belly by the Satanic priestess, an oriental woman. The man

dies, leaving only a handful of photos by which to identify the participants in this murderous mass. They include high-ranking figures in the military and government; one of them, Keeley, is a world-renowned expert in germ warfare. One photo, strangely, has no-one in it.

Torrence, in charge of the investigation, turns to Inspector Murray (seen in the previous film) for advice. Murray in turns recommends the help of Lorrimar Van Helsing, an expert in occult matters. Meanwhile, his secretary is chased by a group of the motorbike thugs, and abducted.

As Van Helsing is told more about the rituals, we see the sacrificed girl apparently come back to life, the wound in her belly healing over. Van Helsing talks of human blood cults. It is here that we are re-introduced to his granddaughter, Jessica; now played by Joanna Lumley, she has become a much more mature, sophisticated young woman since the last film.

Van Helsing – an old college friend of Keeley – decides to visit him to try and solve the mystery. Keeley is a nervous wreck, and reveals he has developed a new and ultra-virulent strain of bubonic plague – the Black Death. As he rants about the triumph of evil, violence and chaos, one of the thugs enters and shoots Van Helsing with a drugged dart. When he awakes, Keeley is hanging dead from the ceiling, and the dishes containing the plague are gone.

Cut to the country house. Torrence's secretary awakes, tied to a bed. Smoke starts to seep under the door. The door finally opens; enter – 36 minutes into the film – Count Dracula. As usual, he hypnotises and then bites her through the neck...

That evening Murray and Jessica visit the country house. As Murray is invited in by the oriental woman, Jessica searches the cellars which are filled with coffin-shaped crates. Here she finds the secretary chained to a wall. As she goes to free her the woman bares the fangs of a vampire and tries to bite her. Now the crates open and several other vampire woman, dressed in red robes, advance on her. Her screams bring the attention of Murray, who manages to drive a stake through the secretary's heart. He and Jessica flee, pursued by motorcycle thugs, and escape over a wall.

The police investigation leads them to the mysterious D.D. Denham, a wealthy industrialist, who apparently owns the country house. Van Helsing is now convinced that the curse of vampirism lies behind the Satanic rituals; he warns Torrence of Dracula – it seems that Denham's headquarters were built on the exact site where Van Helsing last dispatched the Count, two years previously – explaining that the "blank" photo can be accounted for by vampires casting no reflection. He explains the various ways to kill vampires, including a previously unknown one – it seems that the hawthorne tree, which provided Jesus with his crown of thorns, is fatal to a vampire because of this religious association. Van Helsing explains that the approaching 23rd November is also known as the Sabbat of the Undead, and that this date has apparently been chosen by Dracula as the day on which to instigate his ultimate revenge against mankind – Armageddon.

The next day Torrence, Murray, Jessica and Torrence's superior are seen near the country house, keeping it under surveillance. Torrence and his superor are shot dead by snipers, Jessica and Murray captured. Meanwhile, Van Helsing goes to meet the mysterious D.D. Denham., armed with a gun and silver bullet which he has forged from a melted crucifix. Denham remains in shadow, speaking with a foreign accent. He does not seem like Dracula – until Van Helsing slips a bible under his hand and it burns him. Van Helsing pulls out a cross and his gun, threatening to kill the vampire king. Just then Dracula's acolytes burst in and disarm Van Helsing, who is taken away to the country house.

There, Inspector Murray comes to and finds himself in the cellar. The oriental woman approaches, asking him for help, but soon reveals the fangs of a vampire. He manages to repel and stake her, then narrowly avoids the clutches of the other red-garbed vampire women who lurch at him. He turns on the sprinkler system, showering them with clear running water, and they expire in agony. Going upstairs, he finds Jessica lying on the satanic altar, out cold or perhaps in a trance. Enter Dracula, with his acolytes and the captured Van Helsing. Dracula hovers over Jessica's supine body, causing the black altar candles to spontaneously combust. The Count starts to torment Van Helsing, crowing over his "supreme triumph" and announcing that as mankind perishes, Jessica will be his bride. To compound the revenge, Van Helsing will now be one of the four "horsemen' of Dracula's apocalypse, condemned to spread the Black Death. At this point, the acolytes realise that Dracula has duped them – they believed the plague was only to be used as a deterrent – but it is too late. The first phial shatters, and its bearer staggers around the chamber screaming.

Meanwhile, Murray is engaged in a fight with one of the thugs upstairs. The thug is finally electrocuted, causing an explosion which collapses the ceiling and sets fire to the Satanic chamber below. As Murray rescues Jessica, Dracula and Van Helsing struggle. Van Helsing flees into the grounds and then into the nearby woods, pursued by the Count. After a while, Van Helsing finds a hawthorne tree, and hides behind it.

The Count discovers him; his fury overrides caution and he tries to push his way through the hawthorne tree, becoming increasingly spiked and snared by its thorny branches. Finally he falls through the tree, but he has been weakened and his foot is still ensnared. Seeing his chance, Van Helsing grabs a nearby fencepost and thrusts it into the Count's body, driving it home with vicious thrusts. Once again Count Dracula expires, disintegrating into a pile of bones and dust. Van Helsing picks out Dracula's signet ring from the remains – freeze frame – the end.

COMMENT

Attempting to stretch the briefly diverting formula of **Dracula Ad 72** with **The Satanic Rites Of Dracula** (1973), Hammer finally came unstuck. It was the last film in the series – and undoubtedly the worst. To make Dracula into some kind of supernatural super-villain was a fatal mistake. Even Dracula's customary resurrection scene was omitted, and his final demise equally weak. The film was an absurd attempt to marry the Count with a modern Doomsday-type plot, and failed miserably. It was the final insult for Christopher Lee, and he would never again don his famous black and red cape.

FOOTNOTE

Hammer were to produce only one more vampire film. In an even more desperate attempt to weld their traditional themes with new cinema trends, they decided to take Dracula to the East in **The Legend Of The Seven Golden Vampires** (1974). A Chinese monk travels alone to Dracula's tomb, and is taken over by his demonic presence. The idea of oriental vampires was fine in itself, but Hammer's cardinal sin was to include the

Count, thus producing a Dracula film without Christopher Lee. The ever-loyal Peter Cushing returned as Van Helsing, but could not carry the film single-handed, seeming oddly out of place amid the flailing martial arts. The thankless task of following in Lee's footsteps (albeit fleetingly) fell to John Forbes-Robertson, but no-one could have carried it off. The film was not a huge success; Hammer's Dracula, and the rest of the vampires, were finally laid to rest.

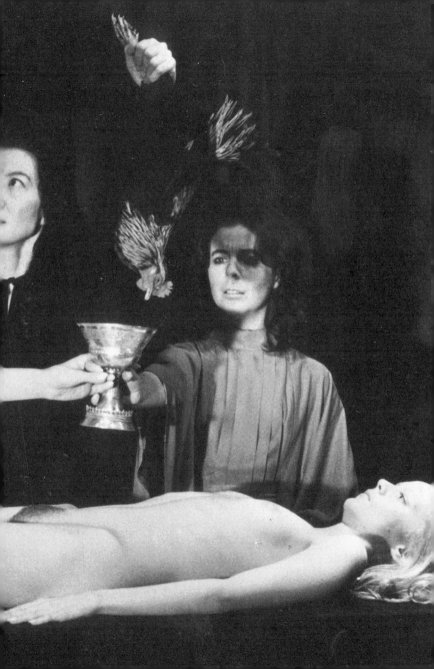

postscript

In retrospect, the seven films featuring Christopher Lee as Dracula clearly form the core not only of Hammer's vampire canon, but of their entire horror output. Despite the different writers and directors involved, and the fifteen years they cover, these films are remarkably uniform in content and texture, far more so than, say, those in the Universal Dracula cycle. Only the Frankenstein series, with Peter Cushing in the recurring role of the Baron, would emulate this consistency within the Hammer oeuvre. The Dracula films – especially those made by Terence Fisher – also best exemplify the classic Hammer dictum, which is that good must eventually triumph over evil. It is this ultimately moral tone which has enabled their films to be accepted all over the world, despite gruesome or blasphemous content.

Count Dracula personifies evil at its most dangerous – when it is fatally attractive. This duality is at the core of Fisher's work, and is usually expressed by the juxtaposition of repressed with uncontrolled sexuality. The male vampire is a perfect embodiment of eros and thanatos, an archetype of the unconscious whose coming augurs all manner of erotic deliria. Dracula's female victims become deranged psycho-sexual cannibals who must be destroyed, purified (hence Van Helsing, the epitome of control and reason, is a celibate), and vampirism is likened to venereal disease. The preponderance of religious symbolism in the films can also be traced back to its carnal origins – the vampire/anti-Christ is rightly repulsed by the holy crucifix, since it is the blood of Christ on the cross which has for two thousand years usurped the power from the blood of menstrual (= sexual) women; like all misogynistic religions, Christianity forever stands between women and awareness of the flesh.

As the Count, Christopher Lee was more than equal to Fisher's demands, and made Dracula into an unforgettable figure – aloof, dignified, austere, yet extremely sexual, and capable of "exploding into tigerish activity when necessary." He refined even the blood-drinking according to his own noble standards. "I nuzzle the victim," he said, "...never kiss her on the lips. Then I mask what follows. It is more effective left to the imagination." The actual bite is never shown; as Lee concluded, "Blood, the symbol of virility, and the sexual attraction attached to it, have always been closely linked in the universal theme of vampirism. I had to try to suggest this without destroying the part by clumsy over-emphasis."

It does seem, in fact, that the dignity of Hammer's Dracula was largely preserved by Lee's attention to the intricacies of the character wherever permitting; he was always aware of Bram Stoker's original character, based on the legendary Vlad Tepes, otherwise known as "Dracul" or "The Impaler", of Wallachia.

"Above all, I have never forgotten that Count Dracula was a gentleman, a member of the upper aristocracy, and in his early life a great leader of men ... you never see me get out of a coffin or resting-place – it would look ridiculous."

Strangely, Hammer seem to have seriously undervalued the importance of their main character; in each of the films Lee himself was to be virtually a bit player – his screen-time actually diminishing throughout the series – having to content himself mostly with dialogue confined to sending the ladies off to devour their boyfriends. In **Dracula, Prince Of Darkness**, his "dialogue" is in fact restricted to a series of animalistic snarls. The screen-time and characterisation afforded Dracula was minimal, with all the attention going on the period characters and protagonists. Perhaps the most interesting ideas were those afforded by the English backgrounds, once the Count had been transported from the limiting boundaries of Transylvania. In **Taste The Blood Of Dracula**, for example, we see the action unfold against a background of Victorian social hypocrisy. The alms house with its biblical quotations on the wall is a cover for Russell Hunter's brothel, and the tyrannically moral father is actually the prime mover in a Hellfire-style vice syndicate. Similarly, we see Christopher Neame as a London swinger in **Dracula AD 1972**, the first of the two contemporary Dracula films scripted by Don Houghton and directed by Alan Gibson, although once again there are only token, cliché'd attempts at drawing on the features of the period. More interesting in this sense is the final film in the series, **The Satanic Rites Of Dracula**, which ironically would have worked extremely well as a straight thriller without the presence of the Count.

It is easy to see why this last film was the final straw for Christopher Lee. His role in the film might have just as well been that of a Fu Manchu or other commonplace villain. One of the few serious working students of Stoker's material, Lee had in fact been dissatisfied with the handling of the Count's character since the very first Dracula, and had been in some dispute with the Hammer executives on the subject. This partially accounts for the seven-year gap between his first and second appearances in the role, although fear of type-casting was probably an equally strong spur. In his third Dracula film, **Dracula Has Risen From The Grave**, Lee disapproved strongly of the scene where the Count removes a stake from his own body. "Everyone knows a stake through the heart is the very end of a vampire," he said. He was over-ruled.

As well as being afforded minimal dialogue, Hammer's Dracula is always over-simplified. Over and over again the writers fall back on a simple revenge plot – culminating in a vendetta against all mankind in **Satanic Rites**. Lee had also felt the need of bigger budgets and more faithful (to Stoker) material – although Hammer had, in fact, created their own running myth of Dracula with each successive film, adding some bits from Stoker, some bits of their own devising. In the first **Dracula**, Lee spent the run of the film confronting Van Helsing, having dispatched Jonathan Harker in the opening third. As in the original Dracula film, **Nosferatu** (1922), daylight kills the vampire. In **Dracula, Prince Of Darkness**, Thorley Walters' Ludwig arrives, a fly-eating maniac derived from Renfield; we are also reminded of Stoker's notion that new vampires need not be bitten by a vampire, but only to drink his blood. It is also shown that clear, running water is fatal to a vampire. We learn of the need to pray over a staking to ensure its efficacy in **Dracula Has Risen From The Grave**, while Dracula finally makes his trip to England – and becomes a more Satanic figure – in **Taste The Blood Of Dracula**. Here, very proximity to the massed icons of Christianity is enough to ensure Dracula's demise. Harker's captivity in Castle Dracula is eventually restaged in the sub-plot of **Scars Of Dracula**, with Lee scaling the castle walls like a human fly in an impressive sequence. He is finally destroyed by fire. **Dracula AD 72** adds a silver blade and holy water to the vampire-killer's arsenal. In the final film, **The Satanic Rites Of Dracula**, the Count is dispatched after being spiked by the thorns of a hawthorne tree.

Perhaps the most significant development throughout the series as a whole is the steady increase in Dracula's stock as a veritable demon from Hell; the rituals required to resurrect the Count become more and more Satanic, the settings for his execrations almost invariably a church of some description, and the methods used to contain him more and more religious in nature, until his status has risen to that of a veritable AntiChrist against whom are ranged the entire physical and moral reserves of Christianity.

Nevertheless, the last word must go to Christopher Lee, for it is his interpretation of the role which made Hammer's Dracula a movie immortal: "I have always tried to emphasise the solitude of Evil and particularly to make it clear that however terrible the actions of Count Dracula might be, he was possessed by an occult power which was completely beyond his control. It was the Devil, holding him in his power, who drove him to commit those horrible crimes, for he had taken possession of his body since time immemorial. Yet his soul, surviving inside its carnal wrapping, was immortal and could not be destroyed by any means. All this is to explain the great sadness which I have tried to put into my interpretation. Audiences, I feel, are more shocked by a sad vampire than a ferocious one."

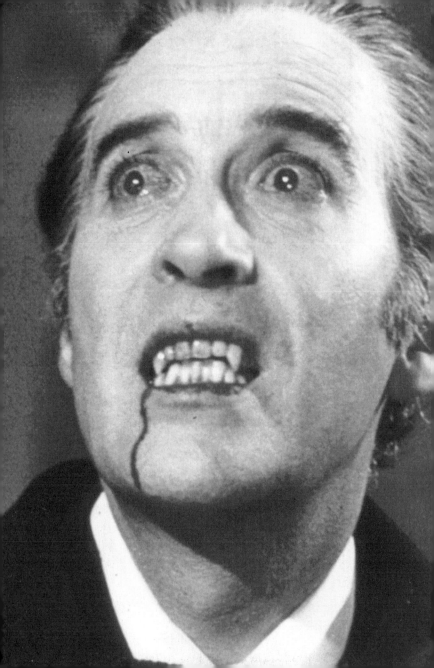